Where's Ray?

Boxer Girl
Illustrated by Morgan Spicer

Order this book online at www.trafford.com
or email orders@trafford.com

Most Trafford titles are also available at major online book retailers.

Print information available on the last page.

ISBN: 978-1-4907-8306-2 (eb)
ISBN: 978-1-4907-8307-9 (sc)

Our mission is to efficiently provide the world's finest, most comprehensive book publishing service, enabling every author to experience success. To find out how to publish your book, your way, and have it available worldwide, visit us online at www.trafford.com

Any people depicted in stock imagery provided by Thinkstock are models,
and such images are being used for illustrative purposes only.
Certain stock imagery © Thinkstock.

Trafford rev. 06/13/2017

www.trafford.com

North America & international
toll-free: 1 888 232 4444 (USA & Canada)
fax: 812 355 4082

Dedication

This book, and all my previously published work, would never exist if it were not for the SUPER talented illustrator, Morgan Spicer. She is gifted with rare artistic talent who undoubtedly stands out from the rest. It only makes perfect sense to dedicate this book to her. I cannot wait to see her next project because she continually amazes me. Thank you for EVERYTHING you do, Morgan!

Acknowledgments

Many thanks to Morgan Spicer who cleverly illustrated this wonderfully creative activities book. Children and adults from all walks of life are sure to love. Also, much love to my family and friends, especially Mom and Dad, who always encouraged me to "Shoot for the Stars!" Is it ironic I have a girl puppy named Star? Don't forget to check out Where's Ray? the book. He will truly make your heart smile!

Where's Ray? Cover (Left)

Where's Ray? Kate & Kenzie with Ray (Right)

Written By Boxer Girl
Illustrated By Morgan Spicer

About the Author

Boxer Girl, aka Kelli-ann Reilly, is a Certified Trick Dog Instructor (CTDI) with Do More With Your Dog! She has shared her home with the boxer breed for nearly 20 years. Tag & Pompeii have proved instrumental towards her passion for tricks. Her very first boxer, Buck, (RIP 04/05/2010) had an uncanny obsession with tennis balls and squeaky toys. In 2003, a 10 week old white male boxer named Tag (RIP 11/14/2016) crept into the picture, then a 16 week old fawn boxer named affectionately after Pompeii, Italy joined the growing crew, now puppies Trick & Star have found their way into Boxer Girl's life. Trick is a red & white male border collie and Star is a white female boxer. Kelli-ann is also a CCPDT-KA through Certification Council for Professional Dog Trainers, a CGC Evaluator through AKC, and ABCDT through Animal Behavior College. You can find more information about this SUPER FUN team at tagpompeiitrickstarproductions.com & domorewithyourdog.com/trickdog.

About the Illustrator

Morgan Spicer is the founder of Bark Point Studio, she is also an illustrator, character designer, animal advocate, ethical vegan, TV/Film Addict and the proud parent of three rescue dogs. Morgan Spicer lives in NYC and has illustrated 15 books while also creating custom animal art for her Bark Point Studio followers, a percentage of these commissions are donated to Animal Rescues and Shelters across the country. It is her ultimate dream to open an Animal Rescue, Sanctuary & Studio [Bark Pointé] to continue educating youth about the magic, friendship, and responsibility that comes with animal companionship. Check out her other works at BarkPointStudio.com

(To the Left)
Up Close and Personal with Tag & Pompeii (Cover)

(To the Right)
Up Close and Personal with Tag & Pompeii

Written By Boxer Girl
Illustrations Morgan Spicer 2015 - 2016

Marshmallow, the Frog asks,
"Can you find my Marshmellows?"

Connect the dots!

Who do you see?

_____

```
U o c I Z V P G V L S Y S K c
M I A V Q L o L L I P o P N W
c A R R o T H R W R W E Y F
F C L B J V L R R U I H R T V
I f M W I B P R S T M B o J L
Z f o o E E P J W I A U N A A
T C G X Q M T K I J R B M Z B
N f S H o o U G N A S B R V U
A Z c K M c L L G U H L R J G
P Z Y T L H I A S F M E T G K
o B E E S A P K E X A G M J B
S M A G I c S E T W L U o D I
T V P Y Z H N K H c L M X L J
E Y c S c I B A c G o o Z Z L
R M K I o P V U M K W E V X H
```

WORD LIST

BEES
BUBBLEGUM
CARROT
LAKE
LoLLIPoP
MAGIC
MARSHMALLoW
MoCHA CHIP
PoSTER
SWING SET
TULIPS

Can you find the differences?

Help Ray find Kate & Kenzie.

Please help Mocha Chip find her carrot!

(Circle the carrot)

Matching

Help Ray decorate Kenzie's cake.
Color by numbers!

1. Red
2. Green
3. Pink
4. Brown
5. Blue
6. Purple
7. Orange
8. Yellow
9. Your pick!

Connect the dots!

What is it? _____

Draw your favorite character!

Help Mocha Chip, Twix and Marshmallow find their homes.

Word Jumble

rhdaybit _____

ePuinat _____

trwea _____

qrirlesu _____

What makes Ray Magical? _____

www.ingramcontent.com/pod-product-compliance
Lightning Source LLC
Chambersburg PA
CBHW041132280526
45792CB00013B/2393